TEACH AND TEST YOUR STUDENTS

Otherwise you may never know
how effective your teaching is
or what they've learned

"If God waited on people to become perfect
before He anointed them
to preach, teach, lead or minister,
there would never be anyone worthy,
and the work would never get done.

God uses willing vessels, with weaknesses,
so His strength, power, and anointing,
can shine through,
and He can get the glory!"

Keith Hammond

Sunday School Teachers
A to Z

Cover Layout and Interior Design: Keith Hammond

Lessons For Life Books

PUBLISHERS

LESSONSFORLIFEBOOKS.COM

LessonsForLifeBooks.com

IMPRINT A Lessons For Life Book

Sunday School Teachers
A to Z

© 2012 by
Keith Hammond
is published by
Lessons for Life Books, Inc.
7455 France Ave. S. #305
Edina, MN 55435

ISBN-13: 978-1-938588-57-0
Library of Congress Control Number: 2012915255
Printed in the U.S.A.

Dedication

God Almighty,
I give you all the glory, honor, and praise for all that you have done
and still do in, to, and through, my life.
Thank you for Jesus Christ and the Holy Spirit,
and for the redeeming power of your Love.

To my wife,
in this 28th year together,
thank you for all your prayers and patience.

To my daughters,
my Love for you goes beyond words.
Many blessings to you both.

To my grandsons,
it is a great joy
to be Blessed with your presence in our lives.

To the Hammond and Fitzpatrick families,
I pray that you will unite arm in arm one day
and allow yourselves to be encircled by
the healing power of God's Love.

To Pastor Arthur Agnew,
only God could know how grateful I am,
for the 10 years you stood by my side.
Your training and teaching and telling will always be with me.

Acknowledgement

Ken E. at MMS,
I thank God for using you to be the springboard
that helped launch this ministry.
Thank you for the open door.
I'm forever grateful.

Dana Lynn Smith
The Savvy Book Marketer
Your wisdom, knowledge & understanding,
are incredible and inspiring.
Thank you for being my coach.

There are others who at some point and time of my life,
made a measurable impact, whether good or bad,
I am thankful for your input into me,
as it helped God prune, grow and mature me in more ways,
than you will ever know.

God Bless You All.

CHAPTER ONE [*Structure*] **19**

   Commission 20

   Mission 21

   Goals 22

   Duties 23

   Attendance 24

   Regular Teachers 25

   Substitute Teachers 26

   Class Schedule 27

   Class Structure 28

CHAPTER TWO [*12 Skills*] **29**

CHAPTER THREE [*Student Recruitment*] **57**

CHAPTER FOUR [*40 Standards*] **60**

Table of Contents

Introduction

This book provides dynamic step-by-step training for Sunday school teachers. Outlines goals, duties, attendance, class policies and procedures, lesson plan tips, info for regular and substitute teachers, class structure, required skills, teacher training, basics of student recruitment, and has 40 simple guidelines to follow such as 'don't assume your students can read'. Every teacher should have these fundamentals of teaching contained in

Sunday School Teachers A to Z.

FROM THE SOURCE

The Bible is God's Word. It is the ultimate and only authority with the power to change people's lives. It is living and breathing, sharper than any two-edged sword. Capable of separating bone from marrow, wheat from tare, sheep from goats.

The Bible is designed to help every Christian grow from infancy to maturity within its 66 books. It was written by men who received notice, inspiration, and direct revelation from God to write down the things they witnessed and experienced to be an example for those who would read the historic record in the future.

On top of that, God added the very thing that also gives us life as humans. He breathed on the words men wrote to make them come alive as scripture (2nd Timothy 3:16).

TEACHING TOOL

The Bible is a teaching tool. God added the opportunity for you to build on the foundation established therein, and expand the lessons into what you need them to be. That's part of the reason it's living and breathing. Things that are alive can be molded and shaped into what is needed for that day, time, hour, subject, category, audience. God included lessons, sectioned by each book of the Bible, from Genesis to Revelation, ready to be copied and used as you need them.

At some point during using the Bible to teach, I would hope that you've gotten the idea to modify the lessons and tailor them to your needs, by adding to what has already been provided. Even if you've never written a lesson plan, developed curriculum, or even created a Bible study from your own research, the process, with the guidance of the Holy Spirit, is rather simple. Select a lesson from the Bible, study the lesson, study it again, and ask the Holy Spirit to give you a list of 7-10 questions that can help you teach your students. Then, locate an appropriate graphic, to complete and present. Regardless of the method you use, I pray that your students will delight in the gift of teaching that the Holy Spirit has imparted to you. And will someday want to be teachers themselves. I love teaching, and I truly enjoy developing materials that God has inspired me to put together to be useful in the Body of Christ for church and ministry. It has long been a passion of mine, and I did it consistently for 10 years that I was in leadership at a local church; and I still do it today.

GROWTH MEASURER

The Bible is designed to incite growth <u>and</u> to measure the growth of your students. The format of the questions you create to include in your lessons plans can not only be used to "teach", but I implore you to use them to "test" your students.

If you have accepted the responsibility of teaching, you will and should be held accountable if they do not grow and mature in your class. I say this because I spent many years observing and years teaching adults who had never grown from infancy to maturity, very simply because they had never been tested on what they knew.

The Bible says growth is mandatory. This is referenced in many scriptures. Why do your students need growth? Many reasons. Such as:

1. To grow and mature into seasoned saints that are equipped to be useful as a solider on the battlefield in the Army of the Lord.

2. To grow to a place in their own walk with Christ where they can be useful to help teach other what they have learned.

3. To grow into representatives of your church and ministry, or their own ministries.

These reasons alone should help you understand the importance of growth. And how vital it is to the overall growth of God's Kingdom. Your responsibility as a teacher is much more and purpose much greater than your local church.

CORRECT THEM

I spent many years observing Bible study and Sunday school classes not only at the church I was in leadership at for ten years, but at other places as well. I learned that based on tradition, teachers will continue to teach things that they know may not be accurate. The stronghold that tradition has over the lives of both teachers and students at some churches, in my opinion, should be broken.

For example, I've heard and witnessed dozens of teachers tell their students that Adam committed the first sin in the Garden of Eden. This is not accurate. 1st Timothy 2:14 teaches that Eve was the one who was deceived and became a sinner. Adam, because of eating what Even had given him, was the vessel that sin was able to enter the world through. Remember, Eve ate the fruit first, but nothing happened. But when Adam at the fruit, God showed back up on the scene, and began to question their actions, doled out punishment, and banished them from the Garden. Another example within this story, is that teachers often teach that it was for "their disobedience" that Adam and Eve were banished from the Garden. Also not accurate. Genesis 3:22 teaches, "And the Lord God said, "Behold, the man has become as one of us, to know good and evil; and now, <u>lest he put forth his hand and take also of the tree of life and eat, and live forever</u>;" Verse 23 says, "<u>Therefore the Lord God sent him forth from the Garden of Eden</u>. "It is vitally important that you study lessons "before you teach them".

CORRECTLY LEAD THEM

In 1997 I gave my life to Christ. However, I spent my entire life in church. Watching, observing, listening to what was being taught. In all the years I've spent in church pews, and in leadership roles over the past 15 years, I've heard the same incorrect teaching about what happens to people when they die. The incorrect teaching is that they immediately go to Heaven. I've heard many pastors say, "I know they're in Heaven looking down on us right now." That's one of the biggest pet peeves I have as a Christian, teacher, writer, author.

Nowhere in the Bible does it say that people immediately go to Heaven when they die. It does say that people like Enoch, Moses, Elijah, experienced going straight to Heaven when God called them, but for those who have "died in Christ" the Bible clearly provides numerous references to "going to sleep" and waiting for the day Christ sounds the trumpet for them to get up out of the grave, meet Him in the sky, and be taken to Heaven, along with the rest of the church that He will come back to harvest. I've heard this taught incorrectly in many classes, and I've even heard it preached during funerals.

I pray it stops.

Why? Because it is my humble belief that if you incorrectly lead one person, they will incorrectly lead another one. And before long, that incorrect teaching has spread to countless others.

EDUCATE THEM

In a Message I delivered years ago to a group of men at a Halfway House titled: 'Grow Into Maturity' I detailed the various levels of growth for most Christians in traditional churches.

What I've witnessed in my experience observing several churches is that most Christians follow this path in their membership:

1. They start as **New Members**.
2. Grow to **Service In The Church**.
3. Grow on to **Serving In The Church**.
4. But often get stuck at serving and never mature enough to become **Leadership In The Church**.
5. And, if they make it to leadership 'in' the church, are often never taught they are supposed to mature on to **Serving Outside The Church**.

So they get comfortable staying within the four walls of the church year after year being taught the same lessons that they have been taught dozens of times before, and the vast majority of students are never taught how to apply what they've learned or the true meaning from Matthew 25:35-36 and James 2:14-26, that faith (church) without works (ministry) is dead. We can have all the Biblical knowledge on the planet, but it means nothing if we do not put it to use. What good is having a brain full of Biblical knowledge if you never use it?

GRADUATE THEM

I have often said to many preachers, teachers and members of churches that the last thing "mature" Christians need is another Bible study, *"if they haven't used what they've already learned."*

What mature Christians need is a ministry study. A ministry study done correctly **graduates** mature Christians so they can represent the church by doing ministry **work "outside the church"**. It trains them how and where to represent the church by feeding the hungry, clothing the naked, visiting the sick, ministering to prisoners, helping strangers, and taking care of widows and orphans. It trains them how to use the gifts of the Spirit in ministry. A good ministry study teaches that we must leave the elementary teachings of Christ and go on to maturity, not being taught the same foundational things about faith, repentance, baptism, laying on of hands, the resurrection, and eternal judgment, as we've been taught before. Hebrews 5 and 6 says we're supposed to mature. Even the 12 disciples reached their level of graduation after being taught for a couple of years by Christ, who then sent them out to apply what they had learned, then told them to come back and report what they had witnessed. I believe, that if churches accurately followed this method of helping its members mature, there would always be a wave of ministry work being done by Christians, in addition to the myriad of social service agencies that have had to pick up the slack to do these things because many churches, and Christians, did not.

ANOINT THEM

After Jesus had trained His disciples, He anointed them, and sent them out to do the work they had been trained to do. He made it clear to them that they should leave his side (meaning get up out of the pews, go outside the four walls of the church, and do some work in ministry).

Luke 9:1 says, "He gave them power and authority to **drive out all demons** and to **cure diseases** and He **sent them out** to **preach** the Kingdom of God and to **heal the sick**."

It is my sincere belief that any church members who have been sitting in the chairs and pews attending Bible Study classes for 10, 20, 30, 40 years, are 'more than ready' to go out and do what they have been trained to do. Why don't they? Simple: Sheep can't lead sheep.

So if the shepherd doesn't open the gate and lead the sheep out of the pen to go and put into practice the training they've received, unfortunately, many of them never will. And they will stay in their comfort zone, by the side of the Shepherd, either to afraid to take the next step, or never being taught that they should. Both, in my opinion are wasteful when you have a church full of seasoned saints never leaving the pen to go anywhere to spread their salt on anyone else. What good is it to be called 'the salt of the Earth' when you keep all the seasoning to yourself? Anoint them so they can anoint others.

RELEASE THEM

Nowhere else on the planet, other than in some churches, can you go to the same class year after year, learning all you can about many subjects, without ever graduating and moving on to the next level.

The problem is, most church leaders and church members believe that there is nothing else beyond Bible Study. Yet, there is.

Again, my statement to many of them has been simply this:

"The last thing a mature Christian needs is another Bible Study. They need a Ministry Study, so they can put into practice what you've already taught them in Bible Study."

Only a handful of church leaders actually get what this statement even means. And even fewer of those have taken any steps toward implementing actual classes for training in Ministry as a graduate school of sorts beyond Bible Study. Why? Because most of the time, one can only teach what one has been taught.

In my book, *"Church On Sunday Nothing On Monday,"* I've included a training curriculum and step-by-step instructions for how to start, implement, teach and conduct a Ministry Study. Jesus taught His disciples this concept from day one. When they were ready to be released, He sent them out to put their training into practice.

INTRODUCTION RECAP

- From The Source
- Teaching Tool
- Growth Measurer
- Correct Them
- Correctly Lead Them
- Educate Them
- Graduate Them
- Anoint Them
- Release Them

These Nine simple principles can and should be your litmus test for how you measure the progress of your students, and also the growth of yourself. Remember, when you were in elementary school and even junior high and high school as well as college, every year that you completed the requirements to move forward to the next grade, you did so. And when it was time to graduate, you did so. Treat your Bible Study students the same way. Elevate them up to the next level.

Here's why: If your Bible Study students were thought of as being in the same type grade levels as elementary, junior, senior high, and college, but were never tested to see where they are, or never made progress to move forward, they would be stuck back in your class year after year. Now imagine an adult being in your kindergarten Bible Study class. Get the picture. That image is totally out of order.

CHAPTER ONE
[STRUCTURE]

COMMISSION

Jesus gave us The Great Commission with a clear and simple purpose. To reach as many people as we can on the planet for the sake of the Kingdom of God.

Growing the Kingdom of God starts with growing your church. Growing your church starts with growing your Sunday school class. It is not a coincidence that Sunday school starts "before" the worship service. It is designed that way. Why? Because Sunday school is the place to gather for one-on-one and group interaction with each other over topics, subjects, and points of discussion, that you may never get the opportunity to speak with the pastor, priest, or bishop about.

Sunday school is the place where you will learn firsthand most of your Biblical knowledge. But hearing the word of God from a preacher is vital to growing your Faith.

Both these infusions of God's Word into your being are to help you become a mature Christian so that once you've sat in the classes and in the pews long enough, you can then turn around and use your gifts to step up and teach, as well as stand up to preach.

The Great Commission needs people to carry is out. And Jesus knew that in order for the people to continue the Ministry that He started, He had to make a way for them to do it.

MISSION

The mission of Sunday school should be to teach God's word to everyone that God provides an opportunity to do so.

This mission is based on 2nd Timothy 2:15, which says...
"Study to shew thyself approved, a workman that needeth not to be ashamed, rightly dividing the word of truth."

The most important thing is that you must love GOD.
The next is that you must follow JESUS CHRIST.
The last is that you must be gifted by the HOLY SPIRIT.

All these things are required in order to be effective teachers.

In order to maintain a standard for Sunday School, teachers must adopt and adhere to standards and protocol. You are there to use your God-given gifts and talents to help edify the church and to carry out our responsibility to teach God's Word.

Sunday school should be a part of Christian education. This book is intended as a guide to everyone involved in teaching Sunday school. Nearly every person has the ability to teach. Once you've sat in the pews long enough, you'll also have something to teach about. Learning is a two-way street. Stay on it long enough and you'll eventually get somewhere.

GOALS

- Help teachers understand that their true gift is in a growing relationship with God and dependence upon Him.

- Help teachers become committed to the Word and to the work of teaching others how to do the same.

- Build relationships that foster growth and development while helping each student recognize and nurture their gifts.

- Help the entire church recognize the importance of Bible teachers and their influence.

- Develop a team of teachers with love for and gifts in teaching the age group for which they are enlisted.

- Provide opportunities that help teachers understand the characteristics and needs of the age group they teach.

- Provide the space, equipment, and materials needed for effective teaching.

- Know students well enough to provide group and individual learning opportunities to meet their needs.

- Help teachers understand and know how to use teaching resources.

- Help teachers to know that the Bible is the textbook, and the curriculum is the tool to help them teach the text.

- Be a positive model of planning and train teachers to conduct effective team planning meetings.

These goals provide a dynamic platform for your teaching and classroom environment and can help you create a checklist of sorts to start with a target mark, and maintain a progress meter to encourage growth along the way. And, you can modify this list at anytime, based on your needs and learning environment.

DUTIES

· Supervise and teach all assigned Sunday school classes.

· Develop curriculum that directly reflects Biblical examples and parallels life today.

· Prepare lesson plans that meet the needs of every age group regardless of the subject.

· Help each individual reach a level of understanding the Word of God by teaching "how to" study.

· Develop training materials that adapts to the ever-changing student population.

· Help all members grow from infancy needing milk to boldness and feasting on the meat of God's Word.

· Work to train others to become teaches so that the work of Sunday school continues to grow.

· Attend all required meetings and training sessions.

· TEST YOUR STUDENTS REGULARLY!!!
· TEST YOUR STUDENTS REGULARLY!!!
· TEST YOUR STUDENTS REGULARLY!!!

The best thing about being an effective teacher is when your student reminds you of something you taught them about what to do when faced with a particular situation.

ATTENDANCE

- All teachers should be in attendance at teacher's meetings the same week they plan to teach in order to teach class.

- At least two teachers should be present at teacher prayer time before class begins on Sunday morning. All teachers should be in their classrooms 5 minutes before start time.

- Each Sunday school teacher shall make contact with absent students each week and keep a record of the contact made in their attendance folder.

- Teachers should try to give 24 hours notice if they are going to be absent. When 24 hours notice is not possible, the teacher should attempt to make contact with someone to inform them of the absence before the class.

- Teachers absent from class with no notice to anyone will not be allowed to teach. The first incident precipitates a warning; the second precipitates suspension for one month; the third is termination.

- Teachers should be in attendance in regular worship services, prayer hours, teacher's meetings, scheduled workshops and training sessions as much as possible.

- Attendance should be managed by a Sunday school Secretary. Any information on class rolls come from there.

*Teaching takes
commitment to God,
to the church,
and to the students.
Without all these,
you will most likely fail.*

REGULAR TEACHERS

- All regular teachers should be members of the church.

- Regular teachers are considered those who are assigned to teach a class.

- Regular teachers must follow the lesson plan given.

- Any material other than the lesson plan must be approved.

- All regular teachers must be accepted by a vote of the majority of the teachers.

- Regular teachers are responsible for the setup, content, space and use of their classroom.

- Regular teachers are responsible for learning what it takes to effectively teach a class.

Put yourself in the shoes of your students. What would you want to learn from you?

Then, make sure that what you learn yourself comes directly from the Word of God.

Remember, It's Not About You.

SUBSTITUTE TEACHERS

Substitute teachers are constantly needed. When substitute teachers are needed in public school, they do not call in an outsider who does not have the skills or the training to teach. That would be unfair to those within the ranks who have the skills and training. Follow the same guideline to continue the regular flow of Sunday school classes:

- The regular teacher is responsible for any class they cannot teach and must ask to assign someone to fill in. The substitute must be within the ranks and must be assigned.

- If no one within the ranks is available to fill in for the regular teacher, then the class without a teacher must be combined with another class. Or,

- Someone outside the ranks who has been pre-approved and the voting majority of regular teachers can be called in to fill in for the regular teacher.

- All substitute teachers must be members of the church.

Being a substitute means just that. You are filling in for a regular teacher.

Follow the lesson, material and guidelines given.

CLASS SCHEDULE

Sunday school classes should start and be dismissed on time. Why?

If your class doesn't start on time, and end on time, guess what...most likely neither will the worship service. Remember, this teaching thing, it's not about you, your schedule, how long it takes to get dressed, get your hair done, makeup on, suit pressed, shoes shined, gas in the car, food in your belly, and a whole list of things. It is about you, being used by God, to teach His sheep, His Word! So move out of the way. Besides, when you're late, you make everyone else around you late. How?

Because other teachers have to stop what they're doing to prepare to carry our their teaching assignment for the day and help your students get some instruction, direction, information, or something that lets them know where you are that morning. Now don't get me wrong, I know things happen. Snow falls, rain pours, roads get slick, and you have to be careful and drive safely so you can get there, even if not on time. That's an excuse! That's right, I said it. Let me spell it. E-X-C-U-S-E! Three reasons, and helpful hints for you.

1. Leave earlier: Do allllll that stuff you cram into your Sunday morning schedule, on Saturday. You knew you needed gas yesterday.
2. Get up earlier: To be a living sacrifice you have to 'want' to be and live like a living sacrifice. Reminder: Teaching class is not about you!
3. Commitment: Even when your students are disruptive, not learning anything, disinterested, distracted, and seemingly bored with your class, teach anyway. God's living Word will handle the rest!

CLASS STRUCTURE

- Adult Classes

  These are designed for individuals over the age of 20.

- Teen Classes

  These are designed for individuals age of 13-19.

- Youth Classes

  These are designed for individuals ages 7-12.

- Children's Classes

  These are designed for individuals under age 7.

*Maintaining a schedule
shows commitment.
If you work a regular job,
most of the time you are required to
come to work at a certain time,
and leave work at a certain time.
And you do it because you know the
consequences if you don't.
Please show the same
consideration to God,
the church, your students,
and to yourself.*

CHAPTER TWO
[SKILLS]

SPIRIT LED

Teachers need to be led by the Holy Spirit. Why? Because it is the Holy Spirit's job to guide us into all truth. John 16:13. Even the Bible in the next verse says of the Holy Spirit that he will not speak of himself, but whatsoever he shall hear.

So, if you want your classes led by someone or something other than God's own voice, direction, leading and guiding, let someone teach your class that doesn't have, isn't connected to, and has no clue as to what the Holy Spirit is.

What you will get is a bunch of lessons from the teacher's interpretation, rather than God's impartation. And yes, there is an obvious and major difference. Here are two clear indications:

ONE:

The first is found in 1st John 4. It says that any spirit that confesseth that Jesus Christ is come in the flesh is of God. So your teachers must be believing it, confessing it, teaching it, and promoting it, to their students, without grumbling, altering, or masking.

TWO:

From time to time, listen and ask the students during your periodic student performance evaluation, if the teacher ever speaks in tongues. If they don't in class, they most certainly should in worship.

Required Skill

Spirit-Led

Teachers need to be led
by the Holy Spirit.

LEARNERS

Your Sunday school teachers should spend lots of time in lesson preparation and constantly studies to acquire deeper Biblical knowledge. Why? Imagine the consequences if they don't.

The Bible says study to show thyself approved, unto God, rightly dividing the word of truth 2nd Timothy 2:15. This is a direct statement to those who intend to teach God's word. We can only teach what we've been taught. And if what we've been taught is flawed in any way, then the transfer of that knowledge will be flawed as well.

God's word is flawless. Proverbs 30:5. And that God that it is. Why? Because if we had to rely upon the teacher who is responsible for helping to impart knowledge of God to their students, but they had not taken time to learn who He is, 'first', not only will the students know it, but that teacher will eventually show it.

The transfer of knowledge from one person to another not only happens directly, but also indirectly, through a process called Osmosis. The way you talk, walk, act, react, and even teach is being broadcast to your students by a medium other than your words and gestures. As a female, the very way you move during class, young women will pick up. As a male, the very way you treat the young women in class, the young men will pick up. So be very careful what, when, and how you do things, because your students are always watching.

Required Skill

Learner

Teachers must
spend time
in lesson preparation
and regular study
to acquire deeper
Biblical knowledge.

GATEKEEPER

Your Sunday school class will always have someone who thinks they know everything. I didn't say they think they know more than you, the teacher. I said they think they know everything. You will meet students who are being influenced by demonic activity in their lives that will do their best to discredit, deter, and even try to dissuade others from even listening to what you have to say about God, Jesus and the Holy Spirit.

This is a distraction, but you, as the teacher, need to know it exists, how to recognize it, and what to do about it.

Being the gatekeeper of your class means that you have a duty that is resting upon the shoulders of someone much greater than yourself. You do not have to do anything but call upon the Name of Jesus in order to bring order to disorder. Why? Demons tremble at that Name. As gatekeeper of the order in your Sunday school class, you cannot rely upon your own strength, might, power, stamina, endurance, or anointing. God is the only one who can give you these things because it is HIS ARMOR that you wear. Reminder: The Battle is not yours. What you are protecting as gatekeeper, is not the truth of God's Word because the Word is alive and breathing and sharper than any two-edged sword. What you are protecting as gatekeeper is the minds of those who could be influenced by the distraction of false teaching or interpretation.

Required Skill

Gatekeeper

Teachers do not allow
any one student
to monopolize the class
so that everyone has a chance
to participate.

And, Teachers certainly
do not tolerate
disruption or distraction
from the intended purpose
of the lesson.

ENCOURAGER

Here's a personal note from my early days of being encouraged. In elementary school I had a coach named Mr. Dizmukes. He was the epitome of how to encourage someone. And made my early acclimation to sports an easy transition.

The first thing Coach did for me my first season of trying out for the basketball team is, he 'watched' me practice. He watched me shoot a hundred jump shots a day. He watched me practice a hundred free-throws and lay-ups a day. He watched me dribble the ball up and down the court with my eyes closed counting the steps so I would always know where I was on the court. He didn't say a word, just watched. This went on for days. At the end of the week he came to me and said, here, take these, wear them, and only take them off to bathe or shower, got it? I agreed. It was a set of leg weights.

Without saying anything, he said everything. After paying attention to what his professionally trained eyes saw, he let his caring heart show. By the end of the basketball season, those leg weights helped me to go from not even being able to touch the bottom of the regulation-sized backboard, to being able, (no strike that), to being 'confident' enough to jump high enough to dunk with my entire forearm inside the rim. Find ways to encourage your students by watching what and how they learn, then use God's heart in you to show it. Simple solution. Lasting impact. Lifelong memories.

Required Skill

Encourager

Teachers offer words
of praise and support
to those in attendance.
It creates
a vibrant atmosphere
so that each student
feels comfortable
and confident
taking part in the class.

REFLECTER

As a teacher, on any Sunday that you teach class, you're with your students for maybe an hour, then the experiences you had for that hour, are in the past.

It is vital that you keep a journal of these experiences during your time as the teacher for this class for several reasons, including:

- To reflect back on how and what you taught.
- To share your journal with those who may teach after you.
- To use it as a way to measure growth for you and the students.

Being one who reflects on what happens in your classroom, with your students, can help remind you of things you need to do going forward. And, as you reflect on the feedback and responses you get from your teaching methods and strategies, again, it can help you discern growth in both your students, and yourself.

Immediate reflection and download of the information you thought about, reminded someone of, or jotted down, into a journal can help you be a better, more informed teacher. I cannot count the times that I used my journal to remind students of something they said, how they said they felt about a certain issue, or just to keep my promise to follow up on something for them, based on a question they asked. My journal helped me be, a better teacher.

Required Skill

Reflecter

Summarizing the feelings,
findings, ideas, and
reactions of the students
after every class is vital.

This material fills the pages
of your journal
that you can keep
and reflect back on,
all year long.
It is a growth measurer.

LISTENER

The neighborhood I grew up in was recently profiled in a national news story by a famous news anchor. The story was about all the gang violence, murders, and lives being lost in that small section of my old neighborhood. I lived that life once. And I could relate to everything the people being interviewed in the story said. Though they said many things, the one central theme and common denominator was evident. "Help us." These words echoed both from the gang members caught up in the microcosm of a do or die mentality that teaches from an early age that you either kill or be killed. Name notoriety is and always has been one of any gang's focus.

The message being broadcast from within the gang summit also made my ears perk up. "No one is listening to us," were the words of many of the young men and women and the parents who lost kids.

Being a Sunday school teacher requires you to listen to your students. If you're dealing with youth as your students, regardless of age, let me remind you that things have most likely changed since you grew up. Two parent homes are no longer common. Living in a shelter during the week and coming to your Sunday school class is likely. So I want to remind you that every one of your students is going through something before they come to your class. So give them the opportunity to speak, then you take time to listen. It is within this framework that you will help them grow and learn how to cope.

Required Skill

Listener

A teacher always pays
close and careful attention
to what the students say
and responds appropriately.
This lets them know
that their insights
and observations
are an important part
of each class session,
that you are listening,
and that you hear them.

CLARIFIER

- Bring Clarity to your classroom.
- Be Clear about your convictions.
- Boost Confidence by being Consistent.
- Concise conversations create Calm.

The students in your Sunday school class will always have questions. Even if they never raise their hand, never want to participate, are afraid to say anything because of what their peers will think or say, they will always still have questions.

Your responsibility as a teacher is to:
- Clearly explain lesson content that may be unfamiliar to them.
- Strive to make each lesson applicable to daily life.
- Ask follow-up questions to make sure students understand the concepts being presented.

Teaching is not difficult when you commit to learning what you teach. This is the only way that you're going to be successful, have an impact on the lives of the students you teach, and be effective in the presentation of your material.

God is always seeking for us to study to show ourselves approved so that we can correctly divide the word of truth into the many chapters, subchapters, categories, examples, and lessons that are needed to teach students in any Sunday school class.

Required Skill

Clarifier

A teacher is responsible
for explaining lesson content
that may be unfamiliar
to the students,
and strives to make
each lesson
applicable to daily life.
A teacher asks
follow-up questions
to make sure
students understand
the concepts being presented.

LEADER

Teachers are the leaders in their classrooms. Lead by example. Live your life striving to be holy and acceptable unto Christ, and teach your students how to do the same. There is no way to hide anything from students who watch every move you make, even outside the classroom. Be the leader you have been called up to be and accept the assignment and responsibility of teaching God's word to unfed, unhealthy, and possibly malnourished minds, with every ounce of gratefulness, thankfulness, and humility.

Teachers are the leaders in your classrooms for a reason. It is God who, through the Holy Spirit, who gives some of us the ability to be teachers (Ephesians 4:11), and we should move forward in the spirit, knowing that God would not give us an assignment, without giving us the anointing to carry it out.

Leadership comes with both responsibility, and reciprocity. This means you are required to give as much as you get from the relationships with your students.

You give them instruction, they give you insight.
You give them training, they give you the ability to see your training works.
You give them a path to righteousness, they give you updates as they walk it.
You give them ground rules for living for God, they give you growth in God.

Walk, talk, think, act, react and all that you need to, to BE the leader.

Required Skill

Leader

A teacher
guides the students
into offering ideas
relevant to their thoughts
and feelings,
about what they are learning.

This gets them engaged
in the class
and can help you identify
who other leaders
may be.

ROLE MODEL

I often hear lots of athletes say they don't want to be role models. The only reason I can think of for them making this statement is that they don't want to be held accountable for their actions. And, they don't want to influence anyone into doing anything. But the reality is, actors, athletes, and others, automatically assume the position of role model the moment they step into the limelight where others are constantly watching their every move. What they wear, others put on. What they say, others repeat. What they buy, others get. When they speak, others listen, and the list goes on and on.

Your duty, as a teacher, is to show your students who the real role model in their life should be, needs to be, and must be. Here are some of the reasons you can use to help your students understand why:

• Earthly role models are people they may never meet.
• Jesus is present in every aspect of their life every day.

• Earthly role models are people who eventually move beyond the limelight.
• Jesus is the Light that illuminates the way down the path to walk.

• Earthly role models are people who will soon die but never for them.
• Jesus died for them. Rose for them. And is waiting in Heaven for them.

• Earthly role models are people who may never stand up for them.
• Jesus is constantly interceding for us and is an ever present help.

Required Skill

Role Model

Serves as a public example
of standards set by Christ
in all aspects of your life.

Additional definitions are
'living sacrifice'
'willing vessel'
and
'living witness'

MEDIATOR

Your Sunday school students will periodically disagree on something. People have their own opinions, interpretations, insights, ideas, and influences. Your duty, as the Teacher, is to separate myth from fact, right from wrong, truth from lies.

Your Sunday school students get their information and their misinformation from a variety of sources including the Internet, books, magazines, television, telephones, radio, and, this next one may shock you, even their own home.

I've had Sunday school students whose parents did not believe, follow, or even acknowledge Christ as their Lord and Savior and did everything they could to constantly berate and put down their kids for even wanting to come to my class. The same will happen to you. I didn't say might, I said 'will'.

In nearly every church in today's society, there are members of the church who attend Sunday school classes without the support of their spouses, parents, or other members of their families. But they still come. They come because they know and understand how vitally important it is for them to have a relationship with God through our Lord and Savior Jesus Christ. They come because Jesus drew them out of whatever situation, circumstance or lifestyle they were in, which may have included some bad choices, and even bad people, to start the process of making a change in their lives. As Mediator, simply always be ready to separate myth from fact, but let the students talk and share what they've been taught in order to correct them.

Required Skill

Mediator

A Teacher brings perspective
on differences of opinion
between class members
and helps the participants
move toward mutual
understanding and respect
no matter
what the issue is.

TENSION REDUCER

In today's society, at no time in our history have societal problems been greater than they are now. And the reality is, that things will get much worse long before they ever get better. Scripture confirms this in many ways.

Your students may be dealing with situations that you have no experience in, training for, or knowledge of. But as their teacher, and most likely the only person they can look to for peace and comfort in their daily life, be prepared to help relieve the tension that can build up in them from time to time.

Imagine what being a 12 year old must be like if you're homeless. You live in a shelter. You go to school, but the laws require the bus to drop you off at its front door. So everyone on the bus, including the kids who don't understand and make fun of you, are aware of your living situation. On top of that, your mom, because your dad is in jail, insists on taking you and your other siblings to church, where you, as a 12 year old, do not yet understand how she can continue to come to a church that doesn't practice what it preaches because if they did, you wouldn't still be homeless. That's one scenario. Here's another. Imagine you're a 15 year old. Your hormones have just helped you realize that all the times you ever said boys are yucky, now have you saying OMG! He is soooooo cute. Now, he's your boyfriend. You've gone way past the first kiss and now you're pregnant. Your parents are Christian and do not believe in abortion, and there is no one else you can talk to. But every week you're in Sunday school class hearing about abstinence. Welcome to the lives of some of your Sunday school students.

Required Skill

Tension Reducer

Teachers remind students
of class guidelines
that keep the class
functioning at its best.

Because each student
may be dealing with
things beyond your control
such as homelessness,
do your best to give them
a proper place and time
to talk to you just to vent.

CORRECTOR

A few pages ago, I made the statement that your Sunday school students get their information and their misinformation from a variety of sources including the Internet, books, magazines, television, telephones, radio, and, this next one may shock you, even their own home. Now, let me add one more: their public and private school classroom.

From the first day any student enters any public and often private school in this country, they are taught lies from the very history books they rely upon to teach them. For example: Columbus DID NOT discover America, but this lie is still printed in every history book in every public school in the country. Why? Because it's easier to continue to perpetrate a lie, than it is to correctly tell the truth about hundreds of years of history, thereby having to rewrite the book, apologize for the lie, and take it on the chin for even continuing to spread that garbage to begin with.

This reality walks into your Sunday school class every week. Monday through Friday your Sunday school students are indoctrinated and fed false information that you are duty bound and responsible for correcting. History books teach that Jesus was simply a prophet, because the laws of the land state that they cannot call Him Savior because it may offend someone else's religion. Forget about inserting your own opinion here, and God knows I had to, because this book would have turned into another hundred pages, but we'll move on and I'll finish this by simply saying, correct that which is incorrect, and let the Holy Spirit guide them into all truth (John 16:13).

Required Skill

Corrector

Teachers are responsible for knowing the Word of God so that they are able to correct students on incorrect interpretations of Scripture.

BONUS REQUIRED SKILL
PERSONAL TESTIMONY

In my lifetime there have been many tragedies. If you've read my story you'd know that from the age of 8 to age 18 there were 10 tragedies within 10 years. As an adult, and more importantly as a born-again Christian, I've spent many years learning to peel off the layers of tragedy and putting on the characteristics of Christ, so that I could forgive, forget, love again, and move forward in my walk with Christ, rather than remain motionless in the land of depression that I was nearly stranded in forever.

Every now and then you need to publicly reflect back on how good God has been to you, in the form of giving your testimony. Your students need to see that you are not only teaching what you believe God can do in their lives, but are a living witness of it.

Giving your testimony can help your students beyond words. There is no way to measure how much of an impact you have on their lives through the sharing of your experiences. I truly believe that God gives us these tests, trials, tribulations, so that when we've come through them that we can help others when our tests become testimony, our trials become triumphs, and our tribulations become tributes!

Testify of the goodness of the Lord and watch the impact!

BONUS REQUIRED SKILL
PERPETUAL TRAINING

Training is mandatory for every teacher who wants to teach God's word. Here are some basic guidelines and standard that you should adopt, modify, use as a model to help teachers be useful and beneficial to God in the best ways possible in their classrooms.

- Teachers should attend training sessions regularly.

- In-House training is done at every teacher's meeting.

- Outside training sessions are done at places such as the National Baptist Convention's Congress of Christian Education every year. Every teacher should attend these sessions. I did for several years, and the benefit is lifelong.

- Training also takes commitment.

- Teachers should be prepared to lead a training session when called upon to share what they've learned.

- Teachers who take the time to go and learn new methods of teaching students benefit in many ways including being able to use what they've been taught so they can teach it.

Sharing new methods of teaching with your students keeps them engaged. If you always teach one way, it will eventually become repetitive and mundane and probably boring. Mix it up. For example: take your Sunday school class on a field trip to the local homeless shelter, let them serve in the food line, then come back the following week and let them share with you their experiences. Engaging students in the real world of Christianity can open their eyes, minds and hearts to God and the Ministry of Jesus in ways yet imaginable.

R e m i n d e r

Here are a few other ways to find books I've written...

www.LessonsForLifeBooks.com
look for our catalog or shop

www.QualityOfLifeBooks.com
search for upcoming titles

CHAPTER THREE
[STUDENTS]

RECRUITING STUDENTS

· The teacher's job is to get students to come to class.

· If you have no students, who will you teach?

EXCERPT WITH PERMISSION

Here's a story from the book,

"What Every Sunday School Teacher Should Know"

As a freshman in college, Jerry Falwell asked permission of the Sunday school superintendent of a local church to teach a class. Young Falwell received a roll book with one name--a junior boy whose attendance in the past had been intermittent.

Falwell was told the class would meet at the end of the hall behind the curtain. For three weeks, young Falwell faithfully prepared his lessons and taught his class of one. It was hard to build enthusiasm to teach only one. As he thought about it, he felt that he or the superintendent had made a mistake. After class one Sunday morning, he offered the roll book back to the superintendent explaining, "this class just isn't going to work."

"I figured as much," the superintendent responded. "I've seen college boys like you before. I didn't think you have what it takes to make it. That's why I gave you that class instead of one of the regular ones."

Young Falwell was embarrassed and angry. He was not used to being talked to that way by anyone.

When the superintendent reached out for the roll book, Jerry pulled it back. "You can't have it," he declared. "That's my class, and I can make it grow."

That week, Jerry Falwell spent most of his lunch hour praying for his class of one and for himself. He asked God to help him make the class grow.

With a single purpose in mind, Saturday morning he picked up his only junior boy and they went to the homes of his one student's friends to invite them to Sunday school.

Then they went to the area parks where junior boys played on Saturday to invite all to come to Sunday school. The next day, new boys attended the class. The next Saturday, Jerry repeated the process, taking the new boys out to find their friends.

Week after week, Saturdays were devoted to visiting the friends of his students to invite them to Sunday school.

By the time his first year of college ended, 54 junior boys were in that class and the superintendent had given them a regular room.

TIPS FOR STUDENT RECRUITMENT

· SPRING SUMMER WINTER FALL
Boys love sports, girls hang at the mall.
Boys are into video arcades, girls get their hair and nails made.
Boys head to the playground, girls go there to hang around.
If you get the boys the girls will follow.
Go on a Saturday because Sunday is tomorrow.
Don't give them much time to ponder or think.
Their attention span isn't much more than a blink.
Offer food and you may get them to stay.
If you get the popular kids, others won't stay away.

I could go on and on with this poem, but I'll let you add your own lines based on the culture and population near you. The poem above is really geared toward places to recruit youth and young adult students. Again, if you have no students, who will you teach?

Reaching adults it different. While younger students will typically follow their parents to church, they haven't formed any sort of negative or biased opinion of the overall church yet, so there's still plenty of opportunity to reach them. Adults on the other hand, may be coming from past experiences with churches, may not want to attend Sunday school because it makes them get to church to early, and on and on. I've heard every excuse. I've learned to use a simple domino effect for recruiting adults to come to class. Tell one, who you know cannot help but tell others. And watch the domino effect. Find another one, repeat. This also works: Each one, reach one. This means that for every one student you have, get them to help you reach one more. Soon, you'll double the size of your class. Have fun!

CHAPTER FOUR
[STANDARDS]

| 1 | **Standard** |

Learn the names of your students

This cannot be overemphasized. You will be able to control your class better and gain more respect if you learn the students' names.

If you have a poor memory for names, take one day to have all the students hold up name cards and take a picture of them to remind you.

Standard 2

Establish authority from the beginning

Expect your students to show respect 100% of the time. Do not let them get away with speaking without raising their hand or not participating when called upon

Deal quickly with inappropriate conduct in a friendly yet firm manner. It will help you establish authority and earn respect.

3 | Standard

Be overly prepared

Use the lesson plan provided for the Sunday School book you use. If there isn't one, create one. Study it, then study it again.

If you're planning activities, you should know how long each activity will take and have an additional activity prepared in case you have extra time.

Standard

4

Find out what students already know regularly!

Testing is an ongoing process. Students may have already been taught a particular point about "It's Not About Me" but only a few of them may have gotten it. But you will never know unless you test them.

Testing your students regularly will help you keep track of what & when you may need to teach a lesson again.

5 Standard

Be knowledgeable about the material

This is vitally important. It includes pronunciation, syntax, and sociolinguistic areas.

You don't have to be a linguist to teach the Bible. Most of what you need to know can be learned from reading guides such as Harper's Guide to Pronunciation.

Standard 6

Be knowledgeable about the student

This is invaluable and can't be said enough. For some students, the only time they will feel love, is in your class.

Take time to learn about the family life of your students in order to understand what they are dealing with before they get to your class and thinking about during it.

7 Standard

Don't assume your students can read

This may be the most important guideline. Learn who can and who can't. This is especially true even for adult students.

If you don't learn this valuable bit of information, you may embarrass them enough to push them right out of class, and maybe out of church.

Standard

8

Don't neglect
the teaching of listening

It is the opinion of many experts that listening is the most important skill to learn how to teach your students. Why?

Because while listening to your students you will learn more about them, than you ever could talking to them.

9 Standard

Use visual aids such as videos to help you teach

As much as possible, try to expose your students to other teachers in a variety of situations.

The best way to do this and the most realistic is through videos. Listening to audio cassettes in the classroom can be helpful, but videos are much more motivating.

Standard 10

Use games & skits in friendly competition.

Many familiar lessons can be teaching tools when turned into games, or activities with a competitive angle.

This is one sure way to engage students, motivate them, get them involved, and liven up your classroom in the process.

11 | Standard

Motivate your students with variety

By giving your students a variety of interesting activities, they will be more motivated and interested, and are more likely to get involved and introduce other students to your class.

Someone said variety is the spice of life; it's certainly true for use in your class lessons.

Standard 12

Don't fail to teach linguistics

As the teacher, it is your duty to learn how to correctly pronounce names, places, things, etc., then teach it to your students.

Otherwise, they'll go from class to class, hearing but never understanding, and teaching what you taught them to others.

13	Standard

Don't fail to teach context

One of the more important aspects of teaching the Bible is putting it in proper context. For example, if you are teaching a lesson on Paul's first visit to Rome, you should learn who the ruler was, type of empire, laws, social and political climate and other things that will make your lesson come to life. Use the 5 W's. (who, what, when, where, why).

Standard 14

Don't leave students in the dark

Explain exactly what they are expected to learn in a particular lesson. Make sure that students know what they are doing and why.

The lessons should be transparent to the students, with a clear organization, reason and structure. This will keep your class flowing well.

15 | Standard

Show interest in the students as individuals

Don't talk down to students. Give them the same respect you expect.

Only then, will true communication take place.

Students have different gifts. Recognize and encourage them in ways that help them learn to use them. And they may end up helping you.

Standard 16

Direct communication between you and them

Students want, more than anything, to talk with the teacher. Don't overteach to the point that they haven't had a chance to interact with you one-on-one.

Allow opportunities for them to be able to come and talk to you about not only the lesson, but anything effective their ability to grasp the lesson.

17 | Standard

Allow time for free communication

Ask questions that allow your students to talk with each other without you being involved in the discussion.

Do however, maintain control. Gauging how they act, react and interact with each other can help you pair teams and groups later on.

Standard 18

Use 'appropriate' humor to liven the class

Make it a habit to get the students to laugh at least once per lesson.

Without laughter, the students may become bored, agitated, disinterested, dissatisfied, distracted and unwilling to continue in a class where a sense of humor doesn't exist.

19 | Standard

Show an interest in the student's gifts

It is vital to utilize your student's gifts in the class. Some don't know they have gifts. You will, when you watch and listen long enough.

Ignoring their gifts may cause them to think you don't value them. Use them periodically as part of the lesson. It will show the students respect and may loosen them up.

Standard 20

Don't have teacher's pets

This is extremely hard to avoid, especially when a student is more outgoing or interested than others.

Nevertheless, try to call on and attend to students as equally as you can. And the way to do this is to create a calendar of whose turn it is to participate in a certain lesson in a certain week. This helps.

21 | Standard

Don't just stand in one spot

Move about the classroom. At times sit with groups and monitor, as well as joining in on the discussion. At times walk about, listen and observe.

You will find this invaluable and will also let the students know you are being observant of any and everything that's going on in class.

Standard

22

Make instructions short and clear

Demonstrate, rather than explaining whenever possible.

Visual learners may not understand your explanation but may tell you they do to keep others from knowing that they don't.

Be aware and adjust accordingly.

23 | Standard

Speak up but don't break eardrums

If the students can't hear you, you're wasting your breath. Not as bad, but still annoying, is the teacher who thinks they must speak loudly to be heard or comprehended. This annoys people to no end.

Especially if you have seniors in your class that have hearing aids. Adjust your voice and try to keep your tone level.

Standard

24

Ask questions to encourage response

Lessons should be student-centered not teacher-focused.

Using your testimony to get a point across is great; but try and encourage interaction as much as possible with as many questions about the lesson as possible.

This process engages students and helps them feel involved.

25 Standard

Don't talk too much

Depending on the subject of the lesson, you should be talking from about 5% to 30% of the lesson.

Again, most lessons should be student-centered, not teacher-focused. The way to let 'them' talk, is simply to ask them questions.

Standard

26

Don't talk too slow

How do you expect your students to understand you if you don't speak at a fairly natural speed?

Oversimplified and affected speech will hurt your students in the long run. Shoot for moderate complexity and more repetition if needed.

27 Standard

Be sensitive
to your students

Watch faces and reactions.
Do they understand you?
Are they interested or bored?

Try to be aware of what is
going on in your classroom at
all times. If you are starting
class and one student is still
talking, try to gently get them
to stop, but do it gently, and
with respect.

Standard

28

Don't be a psychiatrist

Shy, introverted students are not going to change their personalities overnight.

Give these students opportunities to talk in small groups, but don't expect them to shout out answers in front of the class. Take time with them and help them learn to participate more.

29 | Standard

Respect both slow and fast learners

Learning the Bible is not about intelligence or speed; it is about the Spirit.

The important thing to stress to your students is that they strive to improve. And the only way you're going to learn if they are is by testing them on a regular basis. Take more time where and when needed.

Standard 30

Don't lose your cool in any situation

If you do, you will lose hard-won respect. Even if you have to leave the classroom, do it in a controlled manner.

Explain to the class or student why you are unhappy. Put someone responsible in charge. Then, go, pray, find a way to calm your nerves, and return to your class.

31 Standard

Be frank in every situation

Praise your students when they are getting better and encourage them when they are not doing as well as they can.

But by all means, always be truthful and honest with them. They can tell, or they will find out, if you are not being honest about even the smallest things.

Standard

32

Be a coach
in all circumstances

At times you must be more of a coach than a teacher. Push the students to do the best they can.

But sit on the sidelines, as coach, and let your students do what they are being taught to do. They may learn more if you encourage them to seek solution on their own, or as a group.

33 Standard

Be fair and realistic in testing

Teach first and then test. Don't test on subjects that haven't been taught.

Also, remember that the main purpose of teaching is for them to learn. So be patient. This means that when you test, wait for everyone to get it. Take time with those who haven't caught on yet.

Standard

34

Don't overcorrect and don't embarrass

When correcting someone who has said or answered something wrong, be corrective, but don't embarrass them in doing so.

If you think a student can correct their own mistake, don't do the answer for them; allow for self-adjusting, then ask the question, again later.

35 Standard

Take time to reflect after every lesson

Think about your own teaching. After each lesson is over take some time to reflect.

Was the lesson effective? What were the good and bad points? How could it be improved? Did your students learn? Did you explain who, what, when, where, why, and how?

Standard

36

Keep in great mental shape

Teachers don't have to become bored with teaching. Get into it.

Look at new coursebooks and other material for new ideas. Share your ideas with other teachers. Go to conferences, classes, explore the Internet. Do what you have to do to keep your teaching skills up.

37 | Standard

Laugh at yourself sometimes

There are times when nothing goes right in class, despite our best intentions.

We must be humble enough to admit to ourselves and to our students that we just messed up. Your students will grow to respect your honesty and humility. And will learn to do the same over time.

Standard 38

Always be honest your mind will thank you

Put yourself in your student's shoes. Would you want a teacher to lie to you? No!

Remember, the lie you tell today you may not remember next week, and that's just the moment you'll be asked to recall it. Not being able to, may push the student out the door & maybe the church.

39 | Standard

Remember
It's not about you

One of the most important things to remember is that, <u>It's not about you</u>.

Everything, absolutely everything is about God. It all starts with God. It all finds its purpose in Him. And, it's all about Him! Your testimony is "good", but God's testimony is "great"!

Standard

40

Watch for the movement of the Holy Spirit

If one of your students is having an emotional reaction to something in the lesson, listen to how the Holy Spirit wants you to react to it.

Then, allow the Holy Spirit to respond to that need at that time. If you watch closely, you won't miss it! And you'll be more in tun with the Spirit!

Freely Receive...Freely Give

"For where two or three come together in My name, there I am with them."

--Matthew 18:20 (NIV)

Remember: He's always in your classroom.

Contact

Author: Keith Hammond
President
Lessons For Life Books, Inc.
7455 France Avenue South #305
Edina, MN 55435

(952) 884-5498 ofc
(952) 884-3785 fax

author@LessonsForLifeBooks.com

web: LessonsForLifeBooks.com

How to Find Us:

Google:
'keith hammond lessons for life books'

Barnes & Noble:
bn.com
'keith hammond'

Bookwire.com
'keith hammond'

Amazon:
'keith hammond' plus 'book title'

Kindle:
'keith hammond' plus 'book title'

Catalog Reminder:
The best way to get an overall view of the more than 80 books I've written, is to download the full-color, interactive catalog from our website.

LessonsForLifeBooks.com/ catalog.html

Every book page has a link to the preview of that book, and includes ISBN info, ordering info, etc.

IF IT DOESN'T EXIST BUILD IT
*Every Christian Education System
in every church should promote growth.
It should be organized with growth levels
so that students will feel as if they are
accomplishing something.*

*There is nothing worse
than having the same students
in your class year after year
without testing them to see what they know
and elevating them to where they should go.*

Lessons For Life Books

PUBLISHERS

L E S S O N S F O R L I F E B O O K S . C O M

www.ingramcontent.com/pod-product-compliance
Lightning Source LLC
Chambersburg PA
CBHW052140090426
42741CB00009B/2157